ROARING RIDES

LOWRIDERS

TRACY NELSON MAURER

Rourke
Publishing LLC
Vero Beach, Florida 32964

www.rourkepublishing.com

Project Assistance
Ed Newman, AMSOIL INC.

Also, the author extends appreciation to Ralph Fuentes and the staff of *Lowrider Magazine*, Mike Maurer, John Kari, and Kendall and Lois M. Nelson.

Photo Credits: All photos © K-8 images except page 7 © John A. Schrils, Classic Corvettes and page 35 © Barris Kustom Industries

Title page photo: "Laying it low" takes time, skill, and money. Many car owners build their lowriders over several years.

Editor: Frank Sloan

Cover design: Jay Foster

Page design: Nicola Stratford

Library of Congress Cataloging-in-Publication Data

Maurer, Tracy, 1965-
  Lowriders / Tracy Nelson Maurer.
      p. cm. -- (Roaring rides)
Summary: Discusses the history and current popularity of lowriders,
automobiles custom-built low to the ground, as well as lowrider clubs
and car shows, also touching on lowrider bicycles.
Includes bibliographical references and index.
  ISBN 1-58952-748-8 (hardcover)
  1. Lowriders--Juvenile literature. [1. Lowriders. 2. Automobiles.] I.
Title. II. Series: Maurer, Tracy, 1965- Roaring rides.
  TL255.2.M38 2003
  629.222--dc21

                                                      2003010018

Printed in the USA

w/w

LOWRIDERS

TABLE OF CONTENTS

From old classics to new imports,
lowrider cars feature many custom details.

BOW-TIES AND ZOOT SUITS

Ch-ch-bwap. Ch-ch-bwap. Ch-ch-bwap.

Blasting stereos inside brightly painted cars announce the arrival of lowriders like trumpets for the kings. These exotic cars with fancy wheels and pavement-skimming bumpers sound as different as they look.

Different is good to people who own **lowriders**. They treat their custom, or one-of-a-kind, vehicles as works of art.

ART ON A BUDGET

The Great Depression left many people without much money in the late 1930s. The early lowrider builders, mostly young Mexican Americans, didn't let tight funds slow them down. They found creative ways to dress up their cars instead.

Early lowrider builders hid sandbags in the trunks or shortened the rear springs to drop the back end as low as possible. They also rode with fender skirts and shiny hubcaps.

Lowrider builders focused on romance rather than engine performance. Unique style and plush comfort mattered more than speed, especially if a lady chose to ride along.

ROARING FACT

At first, *lowrider* wasn't a nice term. By the mid-1970s, it became a more positive name for the type of car and its driver.

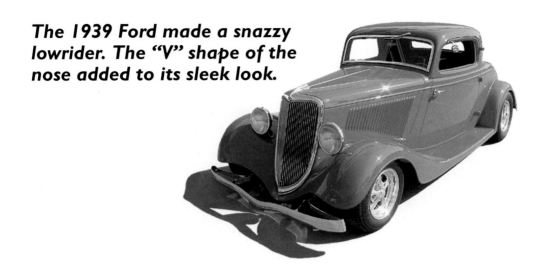

The 1939 Ford made a snazzy lowrider. The "V" shape of the nose added to its sleek look.

CHOPPED-N-DROPPED BOW-TIES

In East Los Angeles, young drivers wanted their cars to look very different from the **California rake** style driven by the wealthier set in West Los Angeles.

The speed-ready California rake dropped low at the front bumper and rode high at the rear on four very wide tires.

The young East L.A. car buffs favored Bow-ties, or Chevrolets, to "chop and drop" into a lowrider. The Chevrolet logo looks like a gentleman's bow tie. Back then, the logo hinted at the extra style the company designed into its early models.

Bow-ties cost less than many other cars of the times. Lowrider vehicles often served as the family car, too. Even today, many lowrider vehicles start as comfortable four-door, full-size cars.

The California rake dropped low at the front bumper and rode high at the rear on four very wide tires. Hot rods, like this Chevrolet Impala, and rakes focused on fast engines instead of fancy interiors.

THE ROAD SHOW

After they chopped down and jazzed up their cars, lowrider builders wanted to show off their mobile art. They also wanted to strut for the girls.

Cruising blended the American passion for cars and parades with a timeless Mexican courting tradition called the *paseo*.

For the paseo, young men walked in one direction around the village plaza while young women walked the opposite way, flirting as they passed by each other.

For the modern version, young men cruised the main streets of *barrios*, or Mexican-American neighborhoods. They drove slowly to flirt with the young women as they passed by.

Lowriders once cruised the streets in several southwestern cities, including Whittier Boulevard in East Los Angeles, California. Now lowrider cars, trucks, and other vehicles attract fans at shows.

THE EAST L.A. STYLE

Drivers often dressed up to cruise around town in their exotic cars. They slicked back their hair. Some wore Hollywood-style zoot suits, which they called drapes.

As time passed, the East L.A. lowrider builders set the standards for custom cars. For a while, they stripped off the factory chrome and filled it with lead or metal from melted coat hangers. The heavy lead made the big, four-door cars even slower. Racy hot rodders in their custom speed machines called the hefty lowrider cars "lead sleds."

Other fads, such as painting the tire rims red, came and went. In time, lowrider builders began keeping all of the factory **accessories** on the car—and they added more swanky parts to zip them up.

Today, imports like this Volkswagen have become more common as builders experiment with different styles.

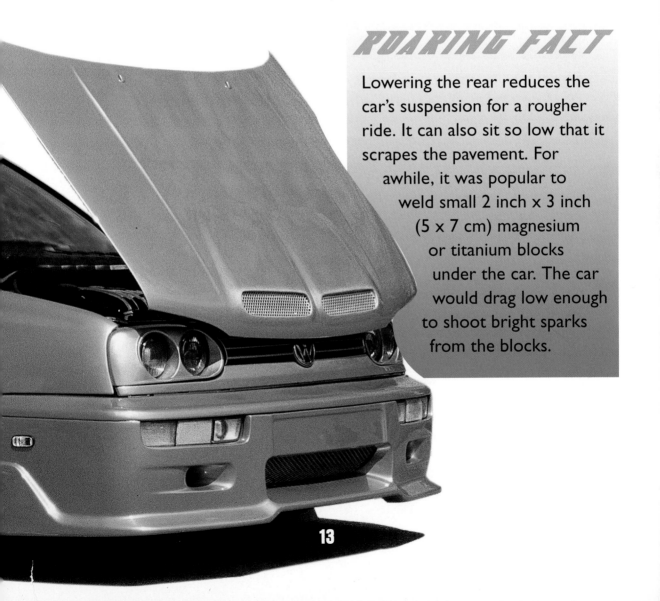

ROARING FACT

Lowering the rear reduces the car's suspension for a rougher ride. It can also sit so low that it scrapes the pavement. For awhile, it was popular to weld small 2 inch x 3 inch (5 x 7 cm) magnesium or titanium blocks under the car. The car would drag low enough to shoot bright sparks from the blocks.

Specialty bumpers, wheels, and other accessories add sizzling style, especially when the ride goes this low!

Trouble followed the early lowriders for many years. Sometimes police hassled the cruisers simply because the drivers came from the *barrios*. Other times, police wisely broke up fights between rival lowrider car clubs. Many cities banned cruising.

Some people saw the lowrider drivers as troublemakers. They didn't see that lowriding actually kept many young adults *away* from gangs. They didn't see the hard work and talent that honest builders put into each of the rolling lowrider masterpieces.

Today, lowrider car clubs work together to promote a better image for lowriding. They share their lowriding traditions. They help kids learn the special skills they'll need to build lowriders. The clubs also bring their communities together.

CHAPTER TWO

HOPPIN' STYLE

California officials passed a law to curb lowriding in the late 1950s. Called Vehicle Code #24008, the rule said only the wheels could sit lower than the tire rim.

Lowriders had loads of experience designing cars without much money. They put the same creative problem-solving skills to work to deal with Vehicle Code #24008. One idea to make the cars **street legal** proved itself in 1959 and pumped up the custom-car world forever.

THE STREET-LEGAL LEGEND

Traditional lowrider builders see Ron Aguirre as a legendary inventor.

The story goes something like this:

Back in 1959, Ron drove a sweet Corvette. The lowered car whisked over the pavement by barely a few inches. Ron needed a way to make the Corvette street legal when he cruised along the California highways.

Ron found a solution by using parts from scrapped airplane landing gear. He changed the airplane **hydraulic system** to fit his Corvette. Then he could raise and lower the car on command.

Today's hydraulic systems allow a car to move up or down in front and back.

The cars also shimmy from side to side.

PUMPS AND DUMPS

The early **pumps and dumps**, or hydraulic systems, could blow out without warning. Lowriders dropped hard in traffic or other dangerous places with deadly results.

Today's custom hydraulic systems feature safety controls to prevent accidents. These gas- or oil-based systems can cost well over $2,000 to install.

One system might include four pumps (shiny with chrome or gold) and four dumps (one for each corner), 6-inch (15-cm) front and 8-inch (20-cm) rear cylinders, one-ton springs, four batteries, and eight control switches in the dashboard.

The switches allow the driver to control the hydraulic movement, such as pumping and dumping the four corners.

Because the complex equipment must fit the car exactly, most owners hire a professional to install the hydraulics.

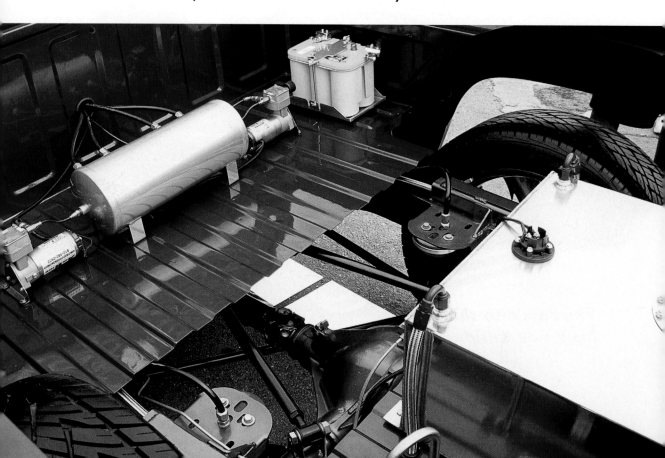

Switches on the console allow the driver to easily control the hydraulic system.

A cut-away bed in this truck lets the judges at a show peek at the precise installation of every part of the hydraulic system.

ROARING FACT

A bank of batteries in the trunk and other hydraulic gear can add more than 500 pounds (226.8 kg) to the vehicle.

DANCE, DANCE, DANCE

    Just as ballerinas move best with a well-tuned orchestra, dancing lowriders jam best with custom sound systems.

    The head unit, or central console, mounts in the dashboard, usually with an **equalizer**, often called an EQ.

    The EQ controls the sound or tone quality. The driver adjusts the EQ for the best sound inside the car. Plush carpets or thick fabrics **absorb** more sound than flat, hard vinyl or plastic surfaces.

The driver might pump up the bass, or low signals, for a plush interior. Or the driver might prefer less treble, or high signals, for a flat interior.

Audio systems must perform as well as the hydraulics. At lowrider car shows, judges check inside the trunks for neatly installed audio systems like this one.

Some sound systems feature a DVD or a CD changer bolted under the driver's seat or wired through the trunk.

An amplifier, usually mounted in the trunk, pumps up the signals from the stereo components. A subwoofer, which is a large bass speaker, also rides back there. Other speakers now come in many shapes and sizes to fit nearly anywhere inside the car.

An audio professional can easily spend more than 100 hours wiring a vehicle's sound system. Many car owners hire a pro to handle the tricky electrical work.

The sound system fills every available space. Speakers come in many shapes and sizes to fit any car.

RIDING IN STYLE

About the same time that the pro installs the audio system, another professional starts working on the interior **upholstery** and other surface coverings.

The best custom carpets and seat covers work well with the audio system. They also echo the exterior design. Often, car owners name their vehicles and choose colors and materials that fit the name.

For example, the "Red Dragon" might have a rich red exterior, red interior upholstery, and even a red-painted engine. Other lowriders feature beautiful murals painted on the hood, trunk, or side panels. Artists paint anything from roses to ghosts for these special cars.

The white flame pattern on the hood sets the tone for the interior. Even the steering wheel echoes the design.

Custom-painted murals on the hood, trunk, or side panels often reflect the car's name or theme.

LOWRIDERS
CHAPTER THREE

TROPHY RIDES

As glamorous and glitzy as any Hollywood event, today's car shows shine and sparkle with hundreds of fabulous vehicles. Even a small-time local show features the artistry, dedication, and talent of lowrider builders.

GLITZ AND GLAMOUR

Major car shows, such as the "Legends" tour promoted by Go-Lo Entertainment and *Lowrider Magazine*, promote friendly competition. Owners display their cars, hoping to win cash and trophy prizes.

Every major show sets its own rules. Most often, judges award points for the vehicle's body, engine, interior, undercarriage, and suspension. The car with the most points in its classification, or class, wins.

Usually, the owners can choose to enter in one of many classes. That way, an all-stock 1955 Bow-tie doesn't compete against a radically modified compact car made in Japan.

Suicide trunks that open backwards or side-opening hoods are just some of the exciting features to see at a car show.

PRIZED BEAUTIES

Just like art in a museum, the cars displayed at a show are
prized beauties from all over the world. Most professionally
managed shows do not allow damaged or **"project cars"**—cars
under construction. They ban vehicles showing ugly gray or
colored primer, the special undercoat that prepares the surface to
hold paint.

Triple-dipped chrome, gold plating, layers of glossy paint, and flashy wheels attract fans to local car shows.

At big-time events, the vehicles may be framed with museum-like red velvet ropes or other clever barriers to prevent guests from touching the works of art. The displays usually look as creative as the vehicles. Mirrors, special lights, and see-through inserts help the judges and fans see every detail on the car.

For fire safety reasons, vehicle owners tape the gas caps and unhook the batteries before an event starts. The local fire department inspects the cars, too, especially for indoor contests.

THE HIPPEST HOP

Lowriders with major hydraulic systems leap and hop in awesome big-air **maneuvers**. Skilled lowrider drivers show off how long and how high their hydraulics can hop. In 1984, one single pump produced the World Record hop at 25.5 inches (65 cm).

Fans cheer for their favorite cars and the best tricks. In contests, car owners stand outside the vehicle and use special controls to make the cars perform.

Hydraulic tricks take lowriding to a new extreme! A skillful driver makes the car hop like it is dancing to music.

The car might bob up and down, nose to trunk, in a move called the seesaw. Another high-skill move is the pancake, which pumps up and then drops down the hydraulics at all four wheels at one time. Hopping the car up and down at each wheel, called the four corners, looks radical, too.

BOMBS AND BIKES

Each car show offers several special prizes. Owners may compete for "Best of Show" for certain groups, including the **Bombs**—American cars or trucks made in 1954 and before.

Many shows also feature motorcycles, bicycles, and tricycles. Amazing accessories, paint, and upholstery create prize-winning two- and three-wheeled rides.

The "Special Interest" class might also include pedal cars, boats, scooters, and almost anything riding low and decked to go.

The entry tag might show the owner's "C.C.," or car club. Car clubs can also take home trophies. They might win for the most members participating in the event or for creating the best club display.

Builders and owners enter their cars in different classes at shows. Notice the sidewinder exhaust pipes on this beauty.

Hovering just above the pavement, this stunning Bow-tie pick-up truck might compete in the "Bomb" class. (The Chevy's bow-tie is on the nose!)

CHAPTER FOUR

MONSTER MAKERS

Lowriders have become famous in songs and movies. Many specialty car fans credit brothers Sam and George Barris with bringing the lowrider style to the American public.

Sam chopped the first hardtop in the early 1950s, creating a sleek profile that looked fast. It wasn't. The brothers also stripped the chrome on that 1951 Bel Air fastback and filled the seams with lead!

THE MAN OF MANY MACHINES

A legendary craftsman, George Barris also promoted his cars with a larger-than-life attitude. He found a market in Hollywood. Superstars, including Elvis, hired him. Movie and television studios asked him to design unique cars for their productions.

Barris created the original "Munster Koach" and "Dragula" lowrider vehicles driven by the Munsters in the 1960s hit television show. The hand-made Koach combined three Model T bodies to stretch more than 18 feet (5.5 meters).

The first Batmobile also came from Barris. He used a 1955 Ford Lincoln Futura concept car as a base. In three weeks, Adam West and Burt Ward took their first ride in the bullet-proof electronic wonder.

ROARING FACT

The Barris Brothers Custom Shop opened in Los Angeles in 1945. The brothers worked with many important car builders such as Bill Hines, who became the pioneer of modern lowrider hydraulics.

Through Barris Kustom Industries, George continues to design rides for the big screen. Watch for his latest project, called *Devil's Knight*.

CUSTOMIZER CLOSE-UP
GEORGE BARRIS "King of Kustoms"

Born: Chicago, 1920s
First Hobby: Model aircraft from scratch
First Modified Car: 1925 Buick
First Custom Car: 1936 Ford
First "K": Kustoms Car Club; he later formed Kustoms of America, which has a major cruise in Paso Robles
First Shop: Bell, California, 1944, with brother Sam
Married: Shirley Nahas, April 25, 1958
Most Famous Rides:

Batmobile, *Batman* TV show
Munster Koach and Dragula, *The Munsters* TV show
General Lee, *The Dukes of Hazzard* TV show
Breathless Roadster, *Dick Tracy* movie
Time Machine, *Back to the Future* movie

Batmobile—Designed by George Barris

TWO-WHEEL LOWRIDERS

Barris took the lowrider style to a new level when he created a bicycle for Eddie Munster to ride on the famous television show. He used the Schwinn Sting Ray, a dragster-like bike wildly popular with American kids then.

Barris added chopper handlebars, a richly upholstered seat, and a dandy windshield to the swoopy Sting Ray. He found a working 19th century lamplight for the front and installed a crash guard as a rear bumper.

Today, a typical lowrider bike features bowed spring-action front forks and spoke wheels—up to 144 spokes on a wire wheel. Importantly, the paint job catches the light and shines with the owner's pride.

ROARING FACT

Schwinn Bicycle Company made about 17 million Sting Ray bikes between 1963 and 1973. The company recently brought the design back again.

Prize-winning bicycles like this two-wheeled lowrider feature amazing designs and details.

MINI MONSTERS

Just as George Barris did in the 1930s, today's young lowriders often start with models. They use kits or build from scratch following a 1/25-inch scale. The tiny hydraulics hop and dance, too!

From small models to small two-door cars, lowriding vehicles take patience and skill to build. Some people simply buy theirs ready-made, like this car for sale at a show.

CHAPTER FIVE

DREAMS ON WHEELS

Lowriders grew from the California Mexican-American community, and its ties remain strong there today. However, people of all races and places fall in love with lowriders. As far away as Japan and Austria, drivers chop and drop their cars with international flair.

Age also doesn't factor into the lowrider world. Kids hang out with their grandparents at car shows and garages. Families cruise together, too.

DRIVEN TO SUCCEED

Many famous people have become supporters of the lowrider scene. Political activist Cesar Chavez built his own lowrider in California in the 1950s. He believed young men and women grew stronger and gained important skills through their lowrider projects.

Car clubs today encourage kids to set goals. Older members help the newest lowriders to earn money and plan budgets for their projects. Building a sweet ride takes a responsible attitude, creativity, commitment, patience, and hard work.

Working on a lowrider can kick off a career in mathematics, physics, engineering, or design. Skills in mechanics, bodywork, or audio installation can open doors, too.

Kids also practice leadership and planning skills when they participate in car club activities. Mostly, they discover they can succeed at their goals!

Car clubs help their members, including kids, learn to build winning rides.

DOWN THE ROAD

Now fueling a $16-billion-a-year industry, the lowriding community sees endless possibilities on the road ahead. More women than ever are joining car clubs and working on their own vehicles.

Car shows continue to attract entries and fans from all over the world. The mainstream automobile world has grown curious and serious about lowriders. Even Public Television recently broadcast a segment about The Dukes Car Club and lowriders.

From California to New York, lowriders have become a vital part of the growing interest in custom cars.

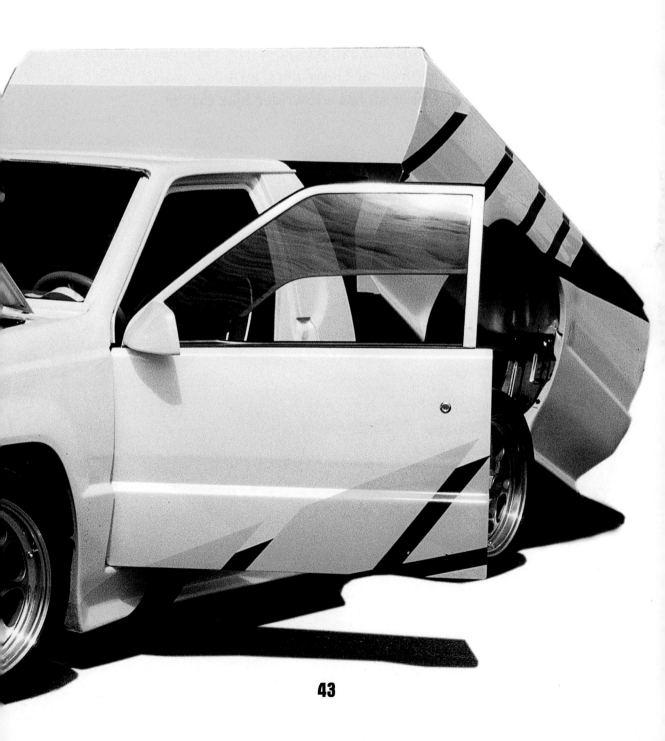

CRUISE INTO THE LIBRARY

As lowriders continue to gain fans, more libraries stock books, magazines, and videos about these custom rides.

Check online for museum exhibits, too. The Petersen Museum in Los Angeles often features rare lowriders, including works by George Barris. Even the Smithsonian has a lowrider bike exhibit.

Further Reading

Low 'n Slow: Lowriding in New Mexico by Jack Parsons and
Carmella Padilla. Museum of New Mexico Press, April 1999.

Lowriders (Enthusiast Color Series) by Robert Genat.
Motorbooks International, October 2001.

Web Sites

Use the keyword "lowrider" to search the internet. Parents and
teachers should note that some web sites might feature
inappropriate content for children.

http://www.lovelylowrider.com/CafamExhibit.htm
Lovely Lowrider Online Resource

http://www.layitlow.com/
Lay It Low Online Resource

http://www.barris.com
Barris Kustom Industries

Glossary

absorb (ab ZORB) — to soak up

accessories (ak SES ah reez) — parts or objects added mainly for looks or effects

bombs (bahmz) — in lowriding, American cars or trucks made in 1954 and before

California rake (kal ah FORN yah RAYK) — a powerful and fast custom car, usually set low at the front bumper and high at the rear on four very wide tires

equalizer (EE kwah liy zur) — in a sound system, an electric device that controls the sound quality or tone

hydraulic system (hiy DRAH lik SIS tem) — in lowriding, equipment that uses pressure from gas or oil forced through narrow pipes to raise or lower the vehicle body

lowriders (LOH riy durz) — custom cars usually fitted with a hydraulic system to lower the car nearly to the road; the person who owns or drives such vehicles

maneuvers (mah NOO vurz) — positions or tricks

paseo (pah SAY oh) — a Mexican courting tradition in which young men stroll in one direction around the village plaza while young women stroll the opposite way

project cars (PROJ ekt   kahrz) — unfinished custom vehicles, usually showing small improvements over a long period of time

pumps and dumps (PUMPS AND DUMPS) — the nickname for the hydraulic systems in lowriders that raise or lower the car body

street legal (STREET   LEE gahl) — a vehicle allowed to be driven on city streets because it meets the standards set by law

upholstery (up HOL stah ree) — the materials, usually fabric or carpet, used to cushion and cover the interior of a vehicle

Index

About The Author

Tracy Nelson Maurer specializes in nonfiction and business writing. Her most recently published children's books include the RadSports series, also from Rourke Publishing LLC. Tracy lives with her husband Mike and two children near Minneapolis, Minnesota.